SWU-NAP- 003

AUSTRIAN ARMY DURING THE NAPOLEONIC WARS 1813-1818

K.K.OESTERREICHISCHEN ARMEE

From the Joseph Trentsensky &
Heinrich Papin artworks
on the Austrian soldiers

SOLDIERSHOP PUBLISHING

Title: **AUSTRIAN ARMY DURING THE NAPOLEONIC WARS 1813-1818**
K.K.Oesterreichschen Armee
Serie edit by Luca S. Cristini. First edition by Soldiershop. September 2018
Cover & Art Design: Luca S. Cristini.
ISBN code: 978-88-93273718
Published by Soldiershop publishing, via Padre Davide, 7 - 24050 Zanica (BG) ITALY. www.soldiershop.com

AUSTRIAN ARMY DURING THE NAPOLEONIC WARS 1813-1818

K.K.OESTERREICHSCHEN ARMEE

THE AUSTRIAN SOLDIER IN NAPOLEONIC ERA

In this book we present the best military artwork of this Wiener-Napoleonic romantic era. more than fifty tables paintings of military subjects as infantry man, cavalry man, artillery, staff and grenzer or specialist troops. The most famous Austrian artist of this era was the Trentsensky brothers that work in conjuntion with the pubblisher Heinrich Papin.
In appendix are also several plates of other most famous Austria/German artist as R.Knotel, Gerash and other from the NYPL collection.

Bildliche Darstellung der k. k. Oesterreichischen Armee

The book, printed in Vienna in 1820, contained the 52 plates of Josef Trentsensky, lithographic works and watercolors of coeval hand, including the title page and the outline of the various military orders, numbered and signed in the plate by Papin. The original book contains a frontspice and a general schema of color uniform for all the armies corp, followed by the wonderful plates, each of which concerns one or more soldiers, with all the ranks discusses separately. The illustrations of the soldiers are coloured in full detail, allowing for an exact reconstruction of the historical uniforms. The binding design is a splendid example of the neo-gothic style of Romanticism.

The artists

Josef Trentsensky (Vienna, 1794-1839). Trentsensky founded with the most famous brother Mattia (1790-1868) a publishing institution specialized in the creation of lithographic printing, which became very popular especially for the "Mandl" series (books for children, illustrated with soldiers of all weapons, civil costumes and drawings of animals, etc.) also developed paper theaters that were very successful. The patent on the "wahrscheinl", a particular wooden bricks was also noteworthy. Invention that was the basis of all subsequent kits for children (up to Lego). Josef worked until his death in the company Trentsensky which in the golden age employed up to 200 workers.

Heinrich Papin (Berlin 1786 - 1839 Vienna), draftsman, miniaturist and lithographer, was the nephew of Daniel Chodowiecki. He lived from 1816 to 1820 and from 1828 in Vienna, where he was the first founder of the Gerold press and lithography factory. He has created numerous lithographed portraits, representations of military uniforms and illustrations for landscape works with folkloristic impact, genre and animal representations.

◀ Equestrian portrait of Kaiser Franz I (1768-1835 by P.J.Krafft

CONTENTS

*

AUSTRIAN K.K. ARMEE DURING THE NAPOLEONIC WARS

The **Imperial and Royal** or **Imperial Austrian** Army (German: *Kaiserlich-königliche Armee, abbreviation „K.K. Armee"*) was the armed force of the Holy Roman Empire under its last monarch, the Habsburg Emperor Francis II, although in reality, it was nearly all composed of the Habsburg army. When the Holy Roman Empire was dissolved in 1806, it assumed its title of the Army of the Austrian Empire under the same monarch, now known as Emperor Francis I of Austria. The ancient name of "Imperial-Royal Army" was used from 1745, as "Royal" referred to the Apostolic Kingdom of Hungary, which was not part of the Holy Roman Empire, but under Habsburg rule. The key feature of the army of the Austrian Empire during the Revolutionary and Napoleonic Wars (1792-1815) was that, due to the multi-national nature of the territories, regiments were split into *German* units (which included Czech-troops recruited from Bohemia, Moravia and Silesia, Polish

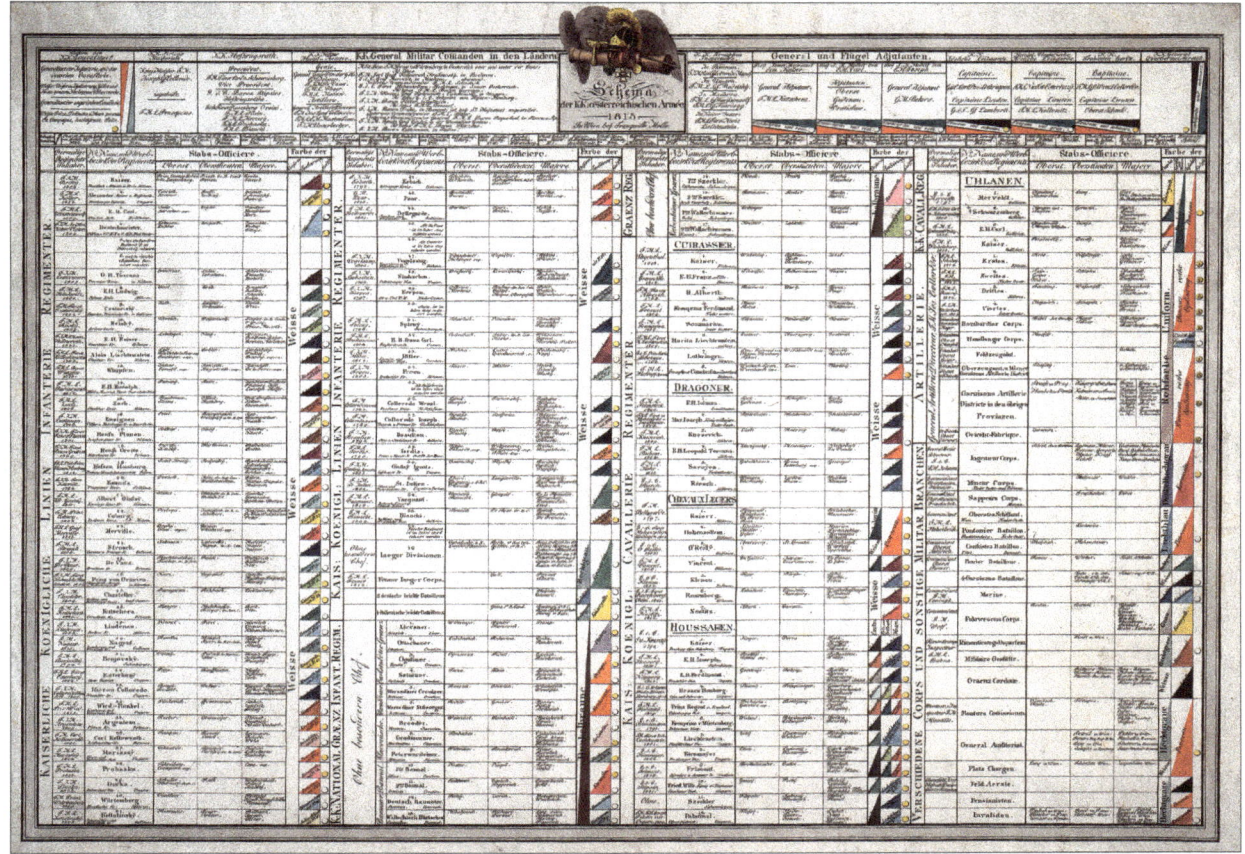

▲ Schema der K.K oesterreichischen Armée 1815.

and Ukrainian units recruited from the territory of Galicia, Flemings and Walloons territory of the former Austrian Netherlands, and Italians) and *Hungarian* units (which included troops from Croatia and Transylvania). Conscription resulted in elements of untrained men in every battalion, a problem exacerbated by incoherent training across the regions.

The army was beset by constant government frugality and several reorganisations. A Militär-Hof-Commission sat for six years from to overhaul the kit, producing the simpler 1798-pattern uniform, the famous crested helmet and a standard musket, copied from the French 1777 pattern. Although some regiments were disbanded in 1809 following the loss of their recruiting-grounds, others were allocated new areas yet kept their old designations. The most powerful individual and famous general in the Army of the Austrian Empire during the period was Archduke Charles, who implemented wide-ranging and modernising reforms, particularly following the crushing defeat at Austerlitz. Charles was responsible for the severe check Napoleon suffered at the battle of Aspern-Essling, but after the subsequent defeat at Wagram retired from active command.

1800 ARMY ORGANIZATION

The first army reorganization of the Austrian army or K.K. Osterreichisches Heer it was based with a new recruiting system and the widening of the duty services, created new units and enlarged the Hungarian troops. After some years of this military adjustment the Austrian army was the following:

Infantry: 63 Line Infantry regiments that include one Jager Infantry regiment and 17 National-Grenzregimenter or Military Border regiments.

Cavalry: 8 Cuirassier regiments, 6 Dragoon regiments, 6 Light cavalryman regiments -- 12 Hussars Regiments, 3 Uhlans regiments.

Artillery: 4 Feldartillerie regiments.

Imperial Guard (Leibgarde)

Staff: (see the table at pag.10 for the military grade)

Engineers: Engineers Corps or Ingenieur Korps: 4 FML, 5 GM, 6 colonels, 8 Lieutenant colonels, 12 majors, 64 captains, 47 lieutenants

Miners or Mineur Korps: 1 Colonel, 1 Lieutenant Colonel, 1 major, 4 captains, 4 lieutenants, 4 Second lieutenant, 1 adjutant, 4 companies of 100 men.

Generalquartiermeister Staff: 4 colonels, 6 lieutenant colonels, 14 majors, 23 captains, 13 lieutenants scattered in the territory, fortresses, major cities, the military border.

Pontooners: 1 colonel, 5 captains, 6 lieutenants, 6 second lieutenant, 11 Oberbrückenmeister (a kind of sergeant major), 6 companies each with 100 men.

Military Train (Milit.rfuhrwesens Korps): 1 colonel, 1 lieutenant colonel, 1 major, 6 Premierrittmeister (first captain), 9 second-rittmeister (2nd captain), 26 lieutenants, 34 second lieutenant, 11 adjutanten scattered in the train (Fuhrwesens) divisions of the major cities.

Remountierung-Besch.lswesens: 2 colonels, 2 lieutenant colonels, 2 majors, 3 rittmeister (scattered among the stations of Mez.hegy.s, Meskowitz, Brandeis, Olmütz, Kolnitz, Vienna and Wels).

▲ The Austrian Arciduque Charles in battle by J.P.Krafft

Kriegskommissariat (War Commissioner): 22 Oberkriegskommiss.re, 72 Feldkriegskommiss.re, 74 Kriegskommissariat officers (scattered in countryland, provinces).

Milit.r-.konomie-Commissionen and Depots (Commissioners for Military Economy and Depots): at Stockerau, Prague, Alt-Ofen (now Budapest), Brünn, Podgorze, Jaroslaw, Marburg, Karlsburg and Vienna (each with 1 Staff officer, 1 captain and 2 lieutenants).

Invalidenh.user (Hospitals for Invalids): Vienna, Prague, Turnau, Pettau (each with a commander, a Staff officer, 1 Auditor, 1 Rechnungsführer, 1 adjutant, 1 arzt (surgeon), 1 kaplan (priest), 1 Kriegscommiss.r).

Military academies: Vienna (Engineers), Wiener-Neustadt (Cadets), Joseph-Akademie of Vienna (medical service), Thierarznei-und Thierspital-Institutof Vienna (veterinary).

Military Police (Wiener Milit.r-Polizeiwache): at Vienna. Mounted and foot "gendarmes". (2 captains, 1 lieutenant and 1 second lieutenant, 1 adjutant and 300 policemen

Military grade	In English name	Note
General officer		
Feldmarschall	Army general	
General der Kavallerie	Cavalry general	
General der Infanterie	Infantry general	
Feldmarschalleutnant	Lieutenant Field Marshal	
Generalmajor	Brigade general	
Senior officers		
Inhaber	Honorary colonel	Used mainly for regiments owned by private individuals, as was the case for the army of the Holy Roman Empire
Oberst	Colonel	
Oberstleutnant	Lieutenant colonel	
Major	Major	
Lower officers		
Hauptmann	Captain	Used for infantry and artillery
Rittermeister	Captain	Used for the cavalry regiment
Oberleutnant	Lieutenant	
Unterleutnant	Second lieutenant	
Cadet officers		
Fähnrich	Ensign	
NCO		
Korporal	Sergeant	
Troop		
Gefreiter	Corporal	Infantry, Hulans and dragoons
Vormeister	Corporal	Artillery
Gefreiter	Corporal	Hussar
Husar	Private	Hussar
Soldat	private	Infantry, artillery and other cavalry

K.K. AUSTRIAN REGIMENTS CHARGES AND RANKS – A DICTIONARY

By Enrico Acerbi

INDEX

Unteroffiziere der kleinen Prima Plana (NCOs of the lesser Prima Plana)
- Feldwebel – Oberjäger - Wachtmeister
- Führer (Zugsführer)
- Sergeant
- Fourier
- Musterschreiber
- Capitaine d'armes (Rüstmeister)
- Feldscher
- Unterärzte (former Feldscher)

Kriegsleute (Gemeine Kriegsleute) (common NCOs and soldiers)
- Corporal
- Gefreite - Patrouillenführer - Vormeister
- Spielleute - (Hautboisten)
- Fourierschütz - Privatdiener
- Zimmermann
- Gemeine

Adjutant
1- Wachtmeister Lieutenant or Regiments-Adjutant
The first time this Charge was observed was in a Verpflegs-Ordonnanz of 1648. He was the "factotum" of the regiment, the right arm of the Obrist Commandant, kept the regiment's lists, the services distribution, diffused the Chief's orders and, in battle, directly defended the Obrist. Dressed like an officer and mounted, he had the rank of the upper Senior Feldwebel. From 1769 his name changed to **Regiments-Adjutant**.

On 1803 they reached the rank of Fähnriche and, on 1807, they had to use a sabre only in face of the enemy and for personal defence. During the XIX century they gradually acquired the mansions of the Auditore and those of the Secretären; from 1861 they received also a governative (Ärarisch) horse for the duty.

2- Bataillons-Adjutant
This Charge was established on 1769, for the kombinierte-Grenadiers-bataillone. They served in the Grenadier battalions in the same way the Regiments-Adjutant served the regiment. During the first Revolutionary wars period (1792-1801) they appeared also in the regular battalions Staffs. This became official (also for the peacetime) after 1803.

Ärzte (Militär Feld-Ärzte) – (surgeon)
1 - Regiments-Arzt (Regiments-Feldscher)
During the Thirty-Years War it became manifest the necessity to have a medical service for the regiment, provided that the company Feldscher was rather unable to manage the complex sanitary matter. Early in 1718 (February 16) a doctor was assigned to each regiment to be the Feldscherer supervisor. In effects the damages, caused by these latter unappropriate or "ersatz" medicine skilled men, began to become very heavy. The Regiments-Feldscher had to be a proven practitioner and was flanked by the companies' Feldscherer with other 10 Feldscher-gesellen (apprentice doctors), who were attached to the Staff. With the prescription (Verordnung) of June 20, 1752 the Regiments-Feldscher changed his name into **Regiments-Chirurg** with the rank (1755) of a young Fähnrich. From 1776 they were also required to know the anatomy and from the Lacy's manual establishment (1769) they reached the Lieutenants rank. On 1803 all the military medical service men received a generic denomination of Feld-Ärzte and the former Chirurg had the new name of **Regiments-Arzt** (Regiments-feld-Arzt), later receiving also the captain's rank, but only in 1854 the medical personnel got the officer full grading and distinctions, only three years before leaving the military Staff to reach one of the new military-parties, the "Sanität".

2 - Ober-Arzt (Bataillons-Chirurg)
The Bataillons-Chirurg born on 1769 in order to give a Chef-Arzt also to the three garrison battalions and to be, eventually, the representative or Stellvertreter of the Regiments-Chirurg. In effects, later, the Hofkriegsrat provided every battalion of its personal doctor. The expression **Oberarzt** (Ober-Feld-Arzt) appeared in 1803, having the doctors to be, like the Regiments Arzt, graduates in Medicine, maintaining, till 1854, either the Oberlieutenant rank, either that of Lieutenant.

3 – Unter-Arzt (Feldscher)

The former Staff's Feldscher-Gesellen in 1769 became unter-Feldscher and had to be skilled in surgery and medicine. These NCOs in 1803 had the name of **Unter-Ärzte**. Till May 1844 their number was fixed in one per division.

Auditor

Or the regiment's bailiff (highest magistrate). He had the task to carry out the regimental trials under command of the regiment commander (Inhaber). He followed also the inheritance affairs of the officers and of every dead man without heirs (in the case of some regimental income, his fee was one Groschen for each Gulden of the inheritance till a maximum tax of 100 Gulden). The Auditore of the infantry had no proper officer Charges; for them the Regiments-Commando created a kind of "Titulatur" equalizing them to an officer's rank. During the first 1700s years (Spanish Succession War) the Auditor collected also the jobs of the Regiments-Secretär (his pay too), so having to manage the regiment's mail traffic and to write the regimental history (also in peacetime), tasks which, from 1807, belonged to the regiments-adjutanten. Finally, on December 18, 1767, the Auditors were authorized (by Inhabern) to be equalized to the rank of Captain. In the Border regiments he had the name of Syndicus and a wage of 200 florins per month.

At the end of the 1700s years the Army restructured the military Justice forming the Militär-Gericht-Wesens. The Auditor became the leader of the Regiments-Auditoriales, acted on behalf of the commander (Inhaber or Regiment commander) and was, at the same time, the official consultant (Referent) of the martial Courts. While before the Auditore could have been removed, changed and nominated by the Inhaber, with the reform they fell under the Hofkriegsrat control. In 1857 they completely lost their military distinctiveness, becaming part of one of the so called Militär-Parteien (military parties or militarised practitioners).

Bataillons-Adjutant

(see Adjutant)

Bataillons-Chirurg

(see Ärzte)

Büchsenmacher

A Charge of the middle '800, officially established on 1852 one for the Regiment's Staff, one for the Cadre battalion. He was a weapons advisor and supervisor (Waffen Offizier).

Cadetten

The term came from the medieval Latin word Capitetum (minor caput = lesser chief), which indicated the not firstborn sons (the minor brothers of an inheritor).

The rank originated from the period 1751-1752 when the Empress Maria Theresia allowed to the officers' sons to enroll in the father's regiment (or in other ones) as cadets. The so called Theresianische Militärakademie was organized by Maria Theresia on 14 December 1751 with the target: *"Mach' er mir tüchtige Officirs und rechtschaffene Männer darauß"* (to form valid officers and correct men). In that military school the Austrian Empire formed its new officers. Officially the rank was introduced on 1763 in two (early) specimens, then in three. Since 1777 they were also called Normale-Cadetten.

    a)   **Fahnen-Cadetten**. They came out from the Theresianische military academy (in Wiener-Neustadt) as the best pupils, directly admitted to first-line charges or as officer's sons come out from the Ingenieurs academy. During the service they were also called K.K. Cadetten. Two of them were assigned to each regiment's Staff, while only one had to remain there, the other being attached to the first (Leib or Obrist) battalion's Staff. Their position was in the battalion's middle, near the flags. The Lacy Regulations of 1769 equalized their rank to that of the young Fähnrich, with the same income. They had to learn how to become officers! An Adjudant or a Wachtmeister-lieutenant was their teacher. This rank lasted till March 16, 1798, when he was abolished by a special act "Allerhöchstes Handbillet" and transformed into the common Fähnrich rank.

    b)   **K.k. ordinare Cadetten**. Also called **Kaisers-Cadetten**, were also pupils in the Theresianische military academy but with a middle scholastic output and mediocre evaluations (not so good to become Fahnen-Cadetten). However, they could have also been simple sons of officers on duty. They were assigned in a number of six per each regiment (to the general Staff) and then were attached one for each company. They must provide to buy uniform and equipment at their own expenses (as the above). With the 1807 Dienst-Reglement this rank was left only to the officers' sons. It will be abolished on 1849 when it will became all Feldwebeln. In effect the Kaisers-Cadetten were all NCOs and were able to had NCOs charges (sometimes definitive too).

c)   **Privat-Cadetten.** With the 1777 Regulations (Normale) it was allowed to each Inhaber to promote valid young men as Cadetten (in addition to the six Kaisers-Cadetten) for NCOs tasks. They reached the NCOs ranks (also definitely) after having mastered the appropriate characteristics of the tasks. During the battle they stood (as the Kaisers-Cadetten) near the flags (Fahnenhauptwache) and guarded them. This rank changed its denomination on 1822 when they were called Regiments-Cadetten.

Capitain-lieutenant

Initially was only a Lieutenant, captain-deputy (Hauptmanns-Stellvertreter) with the provisional company command of a Staff company. Later (1748 Reglement) the rank had its autonomy when was stated each of the four Staff companies must have one Capitain-lieutenant, a rank superior to that of (ober)Lieutenant. After 1805 the Staff assignment ceased. The command ownership of the Staff companies was taken by the Staff officers themselves and there was no more preset numbers of Capitain-lieutenants. This rank was maintained only as a provisional (sometimes honorary) Charge, often in order to led half-companies or detachments. From 1849 the rank disappeared and the Capitain-lieutenants assumed the denomination of 2nd class Captains.

Capitaine d'armes (Rüstmeister)

As the Sergeanten, also the Capitaines d'armes (in French) were part of the company Staffs from the last years of the XVI century (Netherlands war), till the Thirty-years war. They were called also Rüstmeistern, because they overlooked to the weapons and to the ammunitions. However, since the Verpflegs-Ordonnance of 1640, this rank disappeared.

Caplan (Regiments-Pater)

In the Lansquenets armies there was one Feld-Pater per Fählein. He had the same pay of a common "knecht", otherwise he was mounted. Later they were attached to the regimental Staff, in which they never had a military rank. He obviously was the spiritual guidance (Seelsorger) of the troops, leader of his own parish, his regiment. His duties were all the common holy rites and the keeping of the births and deaths records, regarding the regiment. He was named by the Inhaber, under approval of his religious Order, and was mainly subordinated to the Feld-Bishop (Pater Superior), who did not have any part in the nomination, limiting himself to consent it by a letter of approval (Facultäts-brief). The Obrist commander could also punish, if necessary, the Caplan with suspension periods of one-two months, leaving the priest withou pay, without the council of the military bishop.

Since 1769 this ceased to exist and the Fathers were no more under the Oberst's law. The acquisition of the full "privilegii fori Clericalis" (privilege to be evaluated by the Church) had its "verso face of the medal". In facts he lost his wage withe the Gage-Verbot institute, having to be "supplied" only with the minimum necessary to perform his duty.

The distributing Order of January 26, 1771 (Circular-Verordnung) stated the introduction of the so called "Stola-Tax" for the benefit of the religious personnel (Militär-Geistlichkeit). For example, to manage an officer's marriage granted to the Caplan 2 Ducats, to manage a burial 12 Florins and so on.

From 1805, the Caplans were chosen in the "regimental" parish of the bishof's Diocese from which the regiment took its recruits (from 1857 from the Diocese, which the regiment occupied as garrison).

Since the ancient times they all were Catholic priests, the official religion of the Holy Roman Empire. From the Thirty-years War period the army became to accept also the Lutherans or Calvinists, whenever this religions were spread in some regiment. From 1830 it was introduced also the Greek-Orthodox cult, mainly for the former Border regiments, the galicians units and the hungarians ones.

Compagnie (origins)

At the Imperial Diet of 1507 in Worms the structure of a Landsknecht regiment was fully laid out in a document.[1] The structure was a huge step forward in organizational principles, and this document suggests the Austrian Hapsburgs as the founding fathers of the modern regimental structure.

This document gives a structure for a regiment as ten companies (Fähnlein) each company consisting of mixed weaponry being made of forty files (Rotten) each of ten men. The regimental staff was led by the Colonel (Feldobrist) and Lieutenant (Locotenet), also included was a very full support staff including surgeons, priests, Provosts, Adjutant, Quartermaster, and Major (Wachtmeister).

Each company of four hundred men was lead by the Capitain (hauptmann) Lieutenant, and Ensign (Fahndrich), with a Sergeant Major (FeldWebel), Quartermaster (Fourier), Leader (Führer), two Sergeants (Webel) and drummers. The soldiers were known as Gemeine. The soldiers elected a small number of GemeinWebel each month as the lowest level command, it is not clear if their status really equaled the later un-elected Corporals.

Corporal

A Latin word, a latter plural of Caput (head) as capora, from which the Italian Caporale, which the French translated into Corporal, assuming a meaning more close to a (military) generic corps. Today, in Italy, there are rural areas in which seasonal workers squad organizers are called Caporali and their job is referred as Caporalato (in Italy the term often assumes an insulting meaning. The great actor Totò was renowned for his phrase: "Are we men or Corporals?". In the Landsknechts regiments the corporals were called Rottmeistern (the Rott was the early platoon-squad definition). The rank was a NCOs ranks, but not of Prima Plana (namely it did not allow the NCO to voluntary cease his service). In peace the Corporal led a group of soldiers who generally lived together (Corporalschaft), in the time when six Corporalschaften formed a company (a sort of early platoon). In wartime he was the squad-platoon commander (Commandant). His tasks were:

Responsibility about the squad discipline, leading the team training, inspecting the uniforms, equipment and weaponry. He had to be able to speak german, and able to read and write. Moreover he could also led small detachments and Outposts. The more aged Corporal in a company became the "Frei-Corporal" (Gefreiter Corporal), who had not to be confused with the Gefreiter, because he was free also from the common Corporal tasks assuming the charge of a vice-sergeant (Stellvertreter des Führers). During the 30-Years war, the army lists related also of 1st (and 2nd) class Corporals. The 1769 Regulations divided the companies each in four Züge (platoons) (formerly they had four Corporalschaften). In peacetime so there were four Corporalschafts(Zugs)-commandanten, while in wartime the number could raise to two or three per platoon (in which case the elder Corporal was named Zug-Corporal). The more aged from all the coy's Corporals was the natural Feldwebel's substitute (as once happened with the Führern).

This a bit confusing matter ceased in 1857 when the Zugscorporal became the Zugsführer and the Corporals received the control responsibility of the Cameradschaft, with the task to give aid to the Zugsführern.

Erziehungshaus-Commandant

The school-office was established by the Emperor Joseph II on 1782. A subaltern officer was charged to act as teacher instructor for boys. His rank was in the company's list. With him cooperated senior and expert NCOs, while he had the task to explain more ethical matters like discipline and pedagogy. This school offices for "militarized" boys were closed on 1852.

Fahnenführer

During the period in which every company had a flag, this was carried by the Fähnriche. However when these subaltern officers obtained the Lieutenant rank, the flag carrier became a NCO (Führer), and when these latter had to be employed as Feldwebeln, the job was left to another good and senior NCO, called Fähnträger in this function. On 1748 the flag number shrinked to two per battalion, there were 8 Fähnriche and 8 Führern in the regimental Staff. From 1769 the flagbearers were chosen between the eight Führern of the regular companies (since 1763 there were also two regular Fahnen Cadetten, one in the first "Leib" battalion and one in the second "Obrist" battalion, who had to stay near the flags). On 1805, the Führern, were recalled again in the Regiment's Staff (one for each battalion), but only on 1857 they were officially named as Fahnenführern. From 1869, the honour to carry a flag was assigned to the Cadets.

Fähnrich

Literally "Lord of the Flag", the flagman (it. alfiere, lat. vexillarius), was the customer and the guide of the company flag(s). He was the natural substitute of the Lieutenants and directly commanded the Führern. He had to defend the flag until death, had to an example for the other soldiers in battle and was flanked by the band-men (Spielleute). Like the Führern, also the Fähnriche had to visit the sick soldiers in the hospitals, his was the task to overlook the Feldscher's job. In battle had to stimulate the bad soldiers (Delinquenten) and to organize the evacuation of the wounded and died men from the battlefield. The Fähnrich was also called the "company's Mother" (Mutter der Compagnie). Every Sunday and every Holyday he had to lead the Lieutenants to the Holy Mass. The Fähnrich with higher seniority, generally, was that of the Leib-Compagnie. His tasks was the same of the Lieutenants in peace and in war.

During the period 1748-1764 there were eight Fähnriche (two per battalion), attached to the regimental Staff.

On 1769 the task to carry the flags was given to the Führern, while either the Regiment's Staff, either each of the first four regular companies had a Fähnrich. In the battlefield the Fährich was commanded to the flags' guard (Fahnenwache), in the garrisons he was assigned (with flags) to the general or to the main guards (Generals- Hauptwache). Often they were commanded to overlook the hospitals. He was dressed (and payed) like an officer, having, therefore, not only NCO's mansions.

This rank disappeared (for some years) in 1838 and all the Fähnriche became Lieutenants.

Fahrsoldat

A Charge assigned only in war-time. This Charge appeared from 1857 and related to some soldiers of the Regiment's Staff, who had the task of the battle-Train. They were early named as "Fahr und Pack Gemeine" and later "Fahrsoldaten. From 1792 till 1815 this task was assigned to the transport troops (Fuhrwesens).

Feldwebel

Feld=Field Webel=(Wiebel) [2] administrative servant. Was the first NCO of the company in not mounted units and the supervisory for the inner duties in a company. This word comes from the Landsknechte period. Stood in the middle of the battlefield near the Banderuole (Banderols, ancient patrols equivalent of companies – german Fähnlein) in order to transmit the Landsknechte Hauptmann orders, on what the Gemeine had or not had to perform; also administered fees. Near the Feldwebel stood the Stellvertreter der Hauptleute (deputies of higher officers), since then called Lieutenants.

In more modern periods the Feldwebel overlooked at the company organization, made the company's reports, administered the payments for the soldiers, and so on. In German armies the vice-Feldwebel were named Sergeanten or Unteroffizieren and often carried the bataillon's flags. This qualified the rank as similar to a current Sergeant-major. The Feldwebel were selected without taking into consideration seniority, only after the promotion from sergeants and non-commissioned officers. Practically he did, in the company, what the Adjutanten did in the regiment.

Since 1769 they were transferred in the Lesser Prima-Plana lists and so they acquired the right to voluntarily dismiss themselves from service, having a not mandatory Military Duty time.

In the Austrian army, as for the two etymologies, there were Feldwebel and Rechnung-Feldwebel (payments).

Austrian army Equivalents:

Light troops (Jäger) =Oberjäger

Cavalry =Wachtmeister

Artillery =Feuerwerker

Feldwebel in the Napoleonic times as well as before and after, is a rank, he is the highest ranking NCO within a company and there is always only one Feldwebel per company in peacetime. His equivalent in the French army is sergent-major. While in peacetime there was one Feldwebel per company during the wartime, after 1805, each company had one more Feldwebel (a more Zimmermann too). Since November 1, 1849, the second Feldwebel became mandatory also in peacetime, from that time assuming distinctive administrative tasks.

Feldscher

Once upon the time every company had a Feldscher, who had to attend to the sick soldiers, without being, however, a medicine postgraduate or simply skilled in the medical art. For this he was considered a very dangerous fellow. Two times a week he had to shave (and to cut the hairs) the whole company for a minimal fee called the "Beckengeld" (the razor money??). He managed all the drugs like an apothecary and kept records of the expenses. On 1718 it was created the Charge of Regiments-Feldscher, while it was abolished in the companies, where part of the former "barbers" retained the Charge of Feldschergeseller and were subordinated to the Regiment-Feldscher (who now had a Staff duty, treating the higher officers beards).

Regiments-Feldscher

See under Ärzte (Regiments-arzt).

Fleischhauer

A Charge assigned only in war-time. Every regiment had five official butchers, soldiers with this special skill from their civil job. They had a Feldwebel-like rank and directed the troops butcheries. Their direct superior officer was the Proviant-Offizier (commander of the battle Train) and the Fleischhauern, as part of the Train NCOs were also subdue to the Train guard duties. Other infantrymen (Gefreyten) were assigned to them as support or as drivers.

Fourier

The origin of the term is controversial. Someone told it came from the latter Latin Fodrarius (who carried the Fodrum – fodder or forage – for the military animals) (see also the French terms Fourre = straw and so the derivative Fourrier). Other gave it a germanic origin from the two roots for-a-haro (for = vor = before; haro = heer = army), or that man who preceded the army during the march. In effect the first task of a Fourier was to precede his regiment to accommodate camps, lodging and supplies for men and animals.

Initially they had the task of the maintenance and the accounting of the military clothes, directly designated by the captain, and to search and to gather food (bread) and forage, flanking the Proviantmeister (regiment's caterer). He had to organize the quarters, decided by the Quartiermeister, distributing also places (tents) in the camp (Zeltlager). Since the early times he was also employed as orderly by the generals or the regiment's commanders. On 1722, with the Musterschreiber rank abolition, he had also the tasks of the former NCO, i.e. the accounting and the management of the company costs (Rechnungwesen).

Since 1767 they were transferred to the Staffs. Their number was fixed to nine per regiment, being employed each for a division, sometimes one for each company, while the company book-keeping was transferred to the Rechnungsführern. Till 1798 the Fouriere wore the same uniform of the other NCOs; after that year they dressed in grey uniform. In 1802 they had their new uniform, a deep blue overcoat ("caput-Rock"), which turned again in grey on 1808.

From 1849 this rank was progressively abandoned and their duties assigned to the Feldwebeln.

Fourierschütz

Obviously the important tasks assigned to a Fourier needed his personal body-guards. These were the Fourierschützen, in the Landsknechts armies called also Trabanten or Leibschützen. Sometimes they were present in stated amounts (i.e. 12 for the Obrist, 6 for the Hauptmann). During the time evolution, the necessity to act as body-guard began to be less important, so they became the real Fourier's helpers. Under the Prince Eugene rule their number was fixed in four per Company Commander (or Staff officer). There were also other service personnel in the Austrian army called Nachwuchs or Novizen, at that time. On 1726 the number of the Fourierschützen was lowered to two per Company Commander (or Staff officer). On 1767 there was only one Fourierschütz attached as a Fourier's aide. He had to help to find the quarters and expecially the officer's accomodations and services.

On 1771, during the peacetime, every officer and Fahnen-Cadett had one Gemeine at their service. These new Fourierschützen were called **Privatdiener**. They were free from the common military duties, in order to serve the officers. On 1779 also the Auditoren, the Rechnungsführern and the Adjutanten had their Privatdiener. On 1801 all the Staff officers, and the companies commanders (that is also the Capitain-Lieutenants) had a Fourierschütz at their service, while the other higher officers (Regiments-Caplanen, -Ärzte and Auditoren too) had their personal Privatdiener, who had the same wage and uniform [3] as the Gemeine. These soldier were often taken from the invalids or the partialy fit men. (from 1808 they were chosen among the half-invalids of the regiment). The Privatdiener on 1853 received the name of Offiziersdiener and were attached only to Higher and Staff officers.

Führer (after 1857 Zugsführer)

Ancient fuorunga, in „mittelhochdeutsche" füerunge, vüerunge and in XV cent. also voering. One who opens (stay before = vor) the way, guide.[4] A NCO attached to the Feldwebel, who can replace the latter in his command (Stellvertreter of the Feldwebel). In the ancient times (XVI cent.) he had also to be married and able in the art of cooking (this was useful to arrange meals for sick or wounded soldiers). Initially there was one Führer in each company (Fähnlein).

On 1748 they were transferred to the battalion's Staff together with the Fähnrich.

On 1764 they returned in the coy's list (they were the last eight ordinary Führern, those with lesser seniority, to go down to the companies). They had sanitary duties like to visit the hospitalized soldiers, to assist the wounded men a.s.o. They also could have higher commands like those of the flag-guard (Fahnenwache) and the main guards (Hauptwache).

On 1805 they were again transferred to the Staff (see also Stabsführer) and their place was taken by the so called Zugs-Corporalen. On 1857 this rank disappeared and was transformed into Zugsführer rank.

Gefreite (Gefreyte)

When a commander asked a soldier for a special task, this man was free (befreyt) from usual duties and corvées. From the word befreyte (gefreit) came the rank of Gefreite. The Gefreyter originated also from the old Ambosaten of the Landsknechte companies, who had the task to carry the wishes (and complaints) of the Gemeine to their Captains, through their Fähnrich. Since this rank was always considered as honorary they did not receive any additional pay, remaining this the same of the Gemeiner.

They so were soldiers of the Private rank class of the men who, well trained, often the oldest of their squad (Korporalschafts führern), could manage guard jobs as well as leading patrols and other small commands; like provisional Corporals, they were also superior to other soldiers by the time of that special service. They had a little bit higher pay in the German army and carrid "eagled" buttons in the collar and on the shoulders as a badge of rank. The designation was already found before the 30-years war for people, who had distinguished themselves as particularly reliable during the guard duties and when asked to escort the arrested men, therefore, becoming free from military corvée and guard tasks.

In peace the Gefreite was responsible of the good behaviour of his room-mates (Kameradschaft) and controlled the wearing of uniforms, the equipments and sometimes the weapons. They could also become squad commanders with various different task: there were the Zimmerführern or chief of a worker-squad, Cameradschaft Commandanten or lodgement's rulers. In war they coul also become Schwarmführern or patrol commanders. The Gefreiter were also good Stellvertretern (see) or able to replace any NCO charge in the company. Often they inspected (daily) their barracks-rooms and in outer tasks (as guard duties) they often were Aufführern (or vice sergeants), whenever in the smaller outposts they could also command the detachments. They were what the Gemeiner must have as example of a "good soldier".

The lance corporals (Obergefreiten) of artillery directed the guns; they stepped in 1859 in the ranks of the Bombardieren (s. d.). In Austria the Gefreiter was also called: Patrouillenführer among the Jäger, Vormeister in the artillery.

Gemeine

The word today means only generic infantryman. Gemeine was "der Soldat ohne Charge" a soldier without charges, a generic man . The term origins from the Swiss Landsknechte who called the hired men as "gemeine knechte", where Knecht meant an hired hand on a farm or a man who worked with a daily pay. The Landsknechts-Regiment Staff and its companies (Fähnlein) formed a "common" unit called Gemeine (Gemeinde). In this assembly those who did not have special task were called "Gemeiner knechte"

This term Gemeine substituted the term Knecht, during the 30 years war and in the original german regiments, where soldiers were also called "Deutsche knechte", and was often used in contrast with the word "Freiwillige" (enrolled as Volunteer).

On 1701 were formed the Grenadier Companies, in which the Gemeiner changed their name in Grenadier; in the rest of the infantry, the soldiers with the lower income were called also "Fusilier-Gemeiner", but already on 1769, in every army list (Standsliste), the term used was Gemeine.

This term disappeared with the Supreme Resolution (Allerhöchstes Entschliessung) of January 24, 1869 (maybe to avoid a too heavy presence of german words in a new army which was equalized to the Hungarian army by the 1867 Ausgleich). From that moment, in facts, the common soldiers were called as "Infanteristen".

A particular kind of Gemeine was the Zimmermann (see).

Special Gemeiner appeared, in the Austrian army, on 1861 (May 8 Regulation - "Verordnung"). They were:

the **Compagnie-Schuster** or an expert in weapons management and maintenance (for this they had a special Werkzeugstasche or a work-tools sack).

The **Blessiertenträger** or stretcher bearers, fit for Medical service duties.

Hauptmann

(Lat.Med. Capitanus; caput = head of men) (Mittelhochdeut. houbet-man = highest in rank man, the main person. Also associated as heubtman, haubtman). The word was often present as **Kapitän** (Kapitan, Capitain) with the meaning of captain (Chieftain). See under that voice for the word origin and, as for the cavalry captain variant, see under **Rittmeister** (note that, till the end of the XVIII century the Dragoons retained the term Hauptmann for theirs squadrons commanders).

He was the historical company leader and commander (later also of the artillery batteries). Originally he also gave his name to his own company (in the XVII century the captain's son inherited the commmand of his unit and, provided the boy was too young to bring the leadership, this was left to the widow, if any, who was responsible of the payment of her men, as it would be a kind of pension). The heritage of the company troops, in every case, could have been reserved not only to the captains, but also to other formal owners (Eigenthümer) like the Obrist of the first (Guards) company (Leibcompagnie), the Obristlieutenant and the Obristwachtmeistern (been this of some relief for poor widows with no money to hire the men).

By the Lansquenets the Hauptmann stood in the front of his company (Fänlein). He had always to be in close contact with the Colonel in order to manage his orders. This system, having shown to be, in tactics, clumsy and dangerous, was changed with the creation of special officers, similar to the captains, who had the task to diffuse the Colonel's orders leaving the Hauptmann free to command the soldiers. These personal Colonel's aides had the name of Staff officers and could also command special companies called Staff companies. Moreover they often choose to entrust their companies leadership to provisional commanders. So, the regimental Staff companies commanders were generally Lieutenants charged provisionally with the command and called Capitain-Lieutenants.

The captain had also the administrative direction of the whole company (payments, company lists, clothes and equipment). He must organize the discipline maintenance, the exercise and the training of soldiers, had the right of promotions or simply of the promotions proposals, controlled also the punishments and the advancements in rank of his company. The captain had two orderlies at his own service (Fourierschützen or privatdienern).

The captain with the higher degree of Seniority was the official deputy of the Obristwachtmeister, to which he was direclty subordinate and sometimes had the battalion's command, expecily during military parades and battle exercises. Within the years the captain lost the mere function of company commanders and joined the ranks of the higher war commanders (Feldhauptleute).

Hautboisten (Hoboisten)

Literally Oboe players. The English word "oboe" comes from the French word *hautbois* (literal meaning, "high" or "loud" wood. I.e. loud=bass, wood=flute). The term indicated the generic musicians (see Spielleute).

Hilfsarbeiter (Rechnung-Hilfsarbeiter)

Charges established on 1867, mainly of a corporal like rank, worked in the regimental (and Cadre) office (Kanzlei) in order to help the military records and accounting.

Kapellmeister

The military bands were not officially assigned before 1769, time in which the Tambours had the job to revitalize the soldiers with beating drums. Some of the most important (and rich) regiments, however, provided at their own bands. For their management the regiments "hired" music "maestros" in order to direct the wind instrumental bands and sometimes also little string instrumental Orchestras. They had to be Konservatorium graduated. Their rank and wage were stated by the Colonel with a separate contract. One of the most renowned military Kapellmeister was Franz Lehár, father of the famous composer and leader of the IR 50 band.

Kapitän

In 1558, date of birth of the French regiments, the Capitain was a Landslord. Later he became only the owner of the (command of) the company. This meaning of feudal land owner was retained in France. Otherwise the term was largely used in Italy, expecially during the XV-XVI centuries, with the spelling "capitano di ventura" (in Machiavelli, Baldassarre Castiglione and Ariosto) or adventuring captain. This man led an infantry company or a cavalry squadron and was named, later, Condottiero (Lat. conducta = cum ducta or hiring contract). The oldest known "Capitano" was Paoluccio da Calboli of Forlì, son of Fulceri and father of Francesco, who died on 1348. In Germany the term "Capitaneus" was officially taken by the commanders of the cities' garrisons or of some districts (Kreise). In Austria and Bavaria the rank was retained also in the special Guards troops (Arcieren and so on). The Kapitän, in the early times, led also infantry units, but the term was later substituted with the word Hauptmann. It remained in use, however, in the Navy ranks and in the irregular units (insurgents ... also civil teams like in football today).

Kriegsleute (Gemeine Kriegsleute)

Namely men-of-war or battlemen. Die Gemeine Kriegsleute, in the Austrian army, were all NCOs, which weren't of Prima Plana (so they didn't voluntarily retire from duty) and had smaller command to perform. They were:

- Corporalen
- Gefreiter
- Spielleute
- Fourierschützen
- Gemeiner

And from 1861

- Compagnie-Schuster
- Blessiertenträger

Inhaber (Owner, Proprietor)

Or the true regiment's commander (**wirkliche Obrist**). During the first times of the formation of regiments as tactical-administrative units, those (nobles) who could afford the raising of more Fähnlein received a commander approval statement (Bestallungs-Patent), subordinated to their generals (feldobristen or generalobristen) and received the title of Commander of an infantry regiment or Obrist über ein Regiment Fussvolk (zu fuß). Their strong wish of power determined the raising of potent Obristen, who, having the money to do so, organized more than one regiment in order to command their own "little army".

The Austrian Emperor Ferdinand II (April 27, 1624) so was forced to order that one Obrist had to command only one regiment per person. Ferdinand III extended this limitation ordering to the Obristen not committed to the battlefield to abandon the ownership of their regiments (these Obristen were used to leave the command to their Obrist-Lieutenants). At the end of the XVII century, with the general reduction of the armed people in the Holy Roman territories, many Obristen lost their command and were attached to other regiments. So the Austrians created the two historical denominations indicating the true commander as "wirchlich Obrist oder Inhaber" and the attached colonel as "zweiter oder zeitlich Obrist".

During the first 1700s years, the costs to mantain a regiment became very heavy. So there were very few Inhaber able to manage their own units. They resolved to pay only for a part of the regiment, leaving other companies to be raised by free cities or regions. [5]

Under Maria Theresia and, especially under Emperor Franz I it was stated that the ownership of the regiments had to be an imperial matter. The Emperor began to reserve one or more regiment to himself and to give other ownerships to imperial princes (Haus-regimenter) or foreign sovereigns. This new kind of "Obrist-Inhaber" became to be more honorary than effective, often not having the possibility to lead the unit. The imperial nominations ceased the inheritances of the regimental commands. Whenever an Inhaber retired or died the title became without owner or "vakat - vakant" and only after many years, sometimes, the regiment received a new owner.

On 1767, by some regiments where the owner was the Emperor himself or a prince, was instituted the new Charge of "zweite Inhaber" or second owner. This denomination became common till 1817.

All the Inhabern, also the second ones, from 1777 had to be helped by a Inhabers-Adjutant. The owner's Charge became wholly honorary only after the official Act of July 3, 1868.

Lieutenant (Leutnant)

(see also Unterlieutenant - Oberlieutenant) Anciently it was not a rank but a provisional Charge. From the Latin Locus (Fr. Lieu) Tenentis (keeping the place of) it indicated a vice-(someone), a provisional commander who had the command bringing the place of the ordered Commander. In fact there were also Colonels, Generals and Field Marshals Lieutenants. This word became a rank during the Lansquenets period. In the middle of those companies (Fähnlein), ready to substitute the Landsknechte Hauptmann, whenever necessary, stood the Stellvertreter der Hauptleute (deputies of the higher officer, the Captain), since then called Lieutenants.

He was the executive man of the company (like the Feldwebel in more administrative matters and like the Obristwachtmeistern in the regimental Staff), directly subordinating to the captain. Every day he had to inspect the company, to execute the training (or to demand this to the Feldwebel) and to control the company tasks' distribution among the NCOs. He had also to watch rigorously to avoid desertions. Being the captain-deputy (Hauptmanns-Stellvertreter) he often had provisional company commands and when he had to lead a Staff company, assumed the denomination of **Capitain-Lieutenant**.

On 1701, with the birth of the Grenadiers, these elite troops companies lost the Fähnriche, who became a kind of second lieutenant. It was stated to call the former Lieutenants as Oberlieutenants, while the newbies, the former flagmen, were named Unterlieutenants. By 1748 the new ranks of Oberlieutenant and Unterlieutenant were wholly diffused among the army branchs. They were one (each of the two kinds) per company and, together with the Fähnriche, they were called as Subaltern Officiere (Inferior officers).

On 1769 the Oberlieutenant became the second coy's officer, deputy of the captain, while the Unterlieutenant inherited all the former Lieutenants' tasks (inspections, overlooking of the barracks rooms, troop training). These latter, otherwise, had not the tasks to visit hospitals and to manage the flags.

On 1838, disappearing the Fähnrich rank, all the former flagmen became Unterlieutenants. The former Unterlieutenants became Unterlieutenant Höhere Gebühr, while the ex Fähnriche became Unterlieutenants Niederer Gebühr (higher and lower lieutenants). Gradually the prefix unter- was lost in the common military use and the Unterlieutenants became merely Lieutenants, while the use of the term "Oberlieutenant" remained unchanged.

Finally on 1849 the Unterlieutenants were all defined as 1st class (the höherer) and 2nd class (the niederer) Unterlieutenants. The Lieutenant main task was to support the captain in the company duties. They could often be employed as platoon commanders (Zugs-Commandanten). Each company had a number of three Subaltern officers (oberlieutenant, unterlieutenant and a Cadett-Offiziers-Stellvertreter), sometimes had also a Fähnrich, of whom the higher in Seniority was the direct superior rank of the Feldwebel in service. They could also command garrisons and detachments, but having not the same disciplinary rights of a captain (punishments).

Magazins Offizier

In the case the regiment (and its Staff) would have taken quarters in the siege of the Augmentation-Magazine (or at the main recruitment office place - the Werbbezirks-Station) made this task the officer, who was the provisional Proviant-Offizier or a Bataillon Adjutant. At depots (Ersatz-Bataillons-Cadre) a subaltern officer of the military district Staff (Ergänzungsbezirk Offizier) took the same task as acting like Proviant-Offizier in the Cadre battalion. Both had the task to manage the Depot (Magazin), its materials and the Train equipments, having to be present at every drawing away operations into the Depot.

Major (Obristwachtmeister)

In 1600s years they was also called as Regiments-wachtmeisterns. He was the executive man of the regiment. From him all the regiment's orders were diffused. During the training and in campaign he overlooked at the tactical deployment, manoeuvres, pace of marchs, terrain reconnoissance etc. He also organized the alarm deployment of the regiment and the companies (Alarmplätze). He was the supervisor of the guards duties, camps, training, parades.

When battalions became a tactical unit in campaigns [6] they became the battalion's commanders. When the Charge of Obrist regimentscommandant was created, the Major led the first (of three) battalions or the Leib-(Inhabers)-bataillon. The denomination Major came in the middle 1700s (about 1757) together with the word Obristwachtmeister. From the 1807 Dienstreglement this latter disappeared. Since the Seven Years War a regiment had two Majors (a second Major was attached to the Staff). The new standing was established on 1769 and with the 1805 arrangement a third and a fourth Majors were attached to the regimental Staff in order to lead the battalions. From 1807 they became the administrative and disciplinary rulers of the battalions. During the relative peacetime period 1815-1848 the battalions were led: the first, generally attached to the Staff, by the Oberstlieutenant, the second by the 1st Major, the third by the 2nd Major.

The Grenadiers battalions, organized first in 1769, were generally commanded by an Oberstlieutenant assigned by the Hofkriegsrat and in 1790 it was established they must be officers of one of the regimental divisions forming the battalion. From 1815-1848 the Grenadier battalions were led also by a Major (the youngest) of one of the parental regiments. Some Majors (and Oberstlieutenants) were commanded to lead a military district as Ergänzung-bezirk Commandanten. There they were subdue to the Recruitment branch of the army (Heeres-Ergänzungswesens) and part of the territorial forces. In the cavalry they commanded the third division of the regiment (5th and 6th squadrons). Whenever a fourth division was present they led the third (1st Major) and the fourth (2nd major for the 7th and 8th squadrons).

Musterschreiber

Kept the accounting duties of the company, under the direct control of the company commander. He had a NCO rank and could be sent to record the accounts in the main guards or other commands. Since 1722 this Charge disappeared and its task were given to the Fouriere.

Ober-Arzt

See under Bataillons-Chirurg.

Oberjäger

(see Feldwebel)

Oberlieutenant

Oberlieutenant then Oberleutnant = same as Premier Lieutenant (1st Lieutenant). Anciently it was not a rank but a provisional Charge. From the Latin Locus (Fr. Lieu) Tenentis (keeping the place of) it indicated a vice-smtg, a provisional commander who had the command bringing the place of the ordered Commander. In fact there were also Colonels, Generals and Field Marshals Lieutenants. In modern wars the Oberleutnant (Ober= superior indicates always the 1st rank) became the equivalent of the 1st Lieutenant.

On 1701, with the birth of the Grenadiers, these elite troops companies lost the Fähnriche, who became a kind of second lieutenant. It was stated to call the former Lieutenants as Oberlieutenants, while the newbies, the former flagmen, were named Unterlieutenants. (See also Lieutenant).

Oberst (Obrist)

(The highest) commander in the regiment, the Colonel. The true Colonel was the "owner" of the regiment (wirkliche Obrist oder regiments Inhaber), but often he entrusted his command to another Colonel (Obrist Commandant). From the medieval times the Land Lords had the right to create and to pay soldiers for their own services. Over that unit the Lord has the whole rights, like a ruler who acted in the name (and in the absence) of the King, a regent (Lat. regentia

= regency and from regentia came regimentum). This was an individual (Lat. personalis) commitment in war. By the contrary, when the military threat was huge and when the needs for the defence was common to a whole region (Nation?) the commitment became wide-ranging or general (Lat. generalis). So many flags (units, banderia) gathered under a chief who was more important of the colonels (the banderia or regiment commanders). This highest rank was the General-Oberst, from which came the word General.

The Generals distributed the Charges among the Banderia (Obristen) and took the decision whether to group the army in one strong mass or to split it in smaller and quicker forces, with the act of dividing at the origin of the word Division. The divisions, however, were also cause of quarrels between the regiments, in which there were Obristen and Owners, one against the other. We can suppose that, in order to avoid these quarrels (Med.Vulg.It. briga), someone had the necessity to create an intermediary step between the army divisions (many regiments) and the single regiments, with a superior commander, who led two or three regiments and mediated the opinions of the two or three Obristen. It was the birth of the Obrist-Brigadier (very soon changed from individual to general officer or general brigadier) and the fighting group had the name of brigade. [7]

So, at the Lansquenets time, the regiments and the Obristen had only a superior Charge, the Generalobristen. In the Carl V times they had a montly wage of 400 Gulden and were always mounted, with their personal body-guard near the horse (Trabant). They also had the right to name the higher senior captain as their second officer and "Stellvertreter" calling him Obristlieutenant.

At the beginning of the XVIII century, with the increase of the highest ranks (and military careers), the Obristen found more satisfactory to became generals and Fieldmarshals, then to remain bound into their regimental ownerships. It was during the Spanish Succession War (1708?) that this happened for the first time.

The Lords of the regiments abandoned their creatures to other and younger Obristen, who acted only as commander. In the same time the Charge of Inhaber (Owner) became time by time more honorary than heritable, when it meant the true regiment's Owner (who paid soldiers and equipments). On 1755 was officially declared the Charge of Obrist Commandant and till 1805 (like the Owner) he had the rights over a whole company. The Obrist led the regiment afeet on military parades, while in battle was always mounted. In the cavalry they commanded the first division of the regiment (1st and 2nd squadrons).

Oberstlieutenant

As said above, they were the Obristen-Stellvertretern, a rank originally given only to Rittmeistern or Hauptleute. From the XVII century they were a real rank, the second colonel of the regiment (Unterbefehlshaber). They were employed mainly as battalion/squadron commanders. During a period they had also the ownership of a Staff company.

The Grenadiers battalions, organized first in 1769, were generally commanded by an Oberstlieutenant assigned by the Hofkriegsrat and in 1790 it was established they must be officers of one of the regimental divisions forming the battalion. From 1815-1848 the Grenadier battalions were led also by a Major (the youngest) of one of the parental regiments. Some Majors (and Oberstlieutenants) were commanded to lead a military district as Ergänzung-bezirk Commandanten. There they were subdue to the Recruitment branch of the army (Heeres-Ergänzungswesens) and part of the territorial forces. In the cavalry they commanded the second division of the regiment (3rd and 4th squadrons).

Patrouillenführer

Jäger troop Gefreite (see).

[8] Pionier-Corporale

A Charge assigned only in war-time. When regiments acquired a Pionier-Abteilungen (Pioneers sections. Late 1800s) two Pionier Corporals per battalion were attached to those sections. They were common personnel trained in peacetime as technical NCOs, who became Pioniers in war (the soldiers being called as Pionierschülern). One among them had the special task to flank the Pioniers-Abteilung commander (Pionier Offizier) and to perform administrative functions. The Pioneers were the heirs of the Schanzknechte (men o' fortress, also Schanzbauern), the number of whom was stated to be 400 in an army (Fronsberger's Kriegsbuch), distributed in squads (Rotten) of 12 men, led by a Rottenmeister. One Tambour and one Piper lead these squad of men armed with axes and shovels. Wilhelm Dilichi in his Kriegsschule (Frankfurt a. Main 1689) said that "Schanzbauern oder Pionniere" were, in the German regiments, 4-600, sometimes 1000, men per Feldzuge. They had their own captain, 3 lieutenants, 3 Fähnriche, with the axe and hook on the flag, a Tambour but no Piper. They were split in Rotten of 12 men each, armed with picks and shovels.

The Austrian army, otherwise, did not have infantry pioneers till the end of 1700 century. After 1757 was Field Marshal

Lacy to ask for raising an "Arbeiter oder Pioniers Corps". So bore the first Pionier Bataillon (1758), the precursor of the Austrian engineers. After years in which the technical units, raised expecialy in war-times, sometimes enlarged their ranks and in other moments were shrinked down, battalions to Corps and vice-versa to companies-divisions, the official Austrian Pioneers Corps was finally created on January 17, 1809.

Pionier-Offizier

A Charge assigned also in peacetime, from when regiments acquired the Picnier-Abteilungen (Pioneers sections. Late 1800s). This officer had the task to instruct the apprentice Pioneers (Pionierschüler), two Corporals and 16 Gemeiner per each field battalion, which were part of the Regiments-Pioniere-Abtheilung. The instruction was focused on technical works in camps and battlefields. In war he was a subaltern Section commander, while in peace he had also to fulfil company services.

Prima Plana

Prima plana is a Latin term which means „in the first folio". It indicated, in the Austrian army, the ranks which came (were written) first in the army lists or in the first sheet of those lists. These men had the higher wages and marched at the head of the Parade formations. There was also a secondary or lessere Prima Plana which comprised the NCOs. The Prima Plana people had the privilege to voluntary dismiss themselves from military duty as, and when, they did want to do so. The Prima Plana lists regarded company officers and NCOs, which assumed the denomination of Primaplanisten.

Privatdiener

A sort of personal waiter. (see Fourierschützen)

Profoß

The Profoss, Provost or Profot (Dutch "provoost", French "prévôt"), from the Latin "praepositus" (literally prae = before, positus = placed, namely supervisor; term which appeared around 1500) was in the 16th century a military employee instructed about the regiment police, who had to take care, in his regiment, of the diffusion and observance of the field orders under the lansquenets (Landsknechten). Till the 30-years-war the Profoss was assigned to every company or "Fähnlein" and was instructed about the execution of disciplinary punitions. During his service the Profoß was subordinated to the Adjutant in the disciplinary matter, while for his duties he was commanded by the Auditor; he had the rank of a Sergeant. He was also responsible of the treatment of friendly soldiers under trial and of the prisoners of war.

The designation was applied, for example, in the Prussian army at regiment level at least till 1806, while it was maintained in the Austrian army till 1867. Prussian Regiments-profosse had an extremely low reputation and a very inconspicuous, gray uniform. In the army of the separate imperial Districts Profosse had a higher reputation which corresponded to a rather better position of military power. Often they had also the task to search for supplies, to go directly to the towns-markets and to treat the pricing of food and various stuff.

In other german armies (like Saxony) the Profoß had also some subordinates NCOs (Profoßlieutenant, Trabant, Stockmeister) and the so called Steckenknechte, a kind of early military police.

Proviantmeister

Sometimes called also Proviant-Offizier. He managed the regiment's supplies helped by the companies' Fourieren. He also acted as deputy Charge for the Quartiermeister (Stellvertreter) having a rank of inferior officer. The 1769 General Lacy's Reglement introduced a proper number of Proviantmeistern, in order to supply the three battalions during war-times. On 1857 every regiment had a second Proviant-Offizier (a subaltern officer) in war-time (from 1869 also in peace times). In war they commanded the Train of their regiment.

Quartiermeister

He has the rank of the oldest Lieutenant charged to record the regiment's administration. He was a special person, with privileges, who was under command only by only the General-Quartermaster and the Staff officers. He did not fight the battles, acted under the directives of the General-Quartermaster organizing and supplying the camps and the regiment's quarters. The Musterschreiber and the companies' Fourieren were directly under his command. Since 1722 he had, during peacetime, to carry out also the job of the Proviantmeister.

From 1767 this charge was named as **Rechnüngsführer**, with the rank of Oberlieutenant. His tasks remained the same, helped by many Fouriere. The 1769 Reglement established he had to be a proven expert in accounting and totally not self-serving. From 1808 he was equalized to the captain rank.

Rechnüngsführer

(see Quartiermeister) Official Charge from 1767, practically the new name of the Quartiermeister.

Regiments-Privilegien (of the Ownership)

1- the Owner was the supreme judge (Gerichtsherr) of the regiment. He had the rights of the Justice in punishment and in clemency (Lat. Jus gladii et aggratiandi), even deciding the dismission or death of the guilts. This sometimes caused some difficulties in order to establish who could again examine the trials (appeals courts), whether the Emperor himself or the Hofkriegsrat; even in the case the Inhaber was the Emperor himself (infantry regiment n. 1), who could ever contest H.M. Judgements?

However, time by time, this medieval right faded out. First were the officers to became exempted from this system. On 1769 the Gerichtsherr could judge only Gefreyten and Gemeinen. Finally on 1868, this right was transferred from the Inhabern to the brigade-generals. The Obristen commanders did not have this right, unless an official decree would have established it.

2- the Owner had the right to order the promotion and advancements in ranks (Bestallungs- und Beförderungsrecht). From 1766, however, the promotions of the Staff officers were decided by the Hofkriegsrat (and from 1848 by the Emperor). The NCOs promotions were matter of the company commanders, through the approval of the regiment's command.

3- the Owner had the right to concede his approval to the officers and soldiers marriages. On 1769 it was ruled a restricted norm (Heiraths-Cautionen) for not allowing too many marriages by the NCOs and troopers (it was allowed that only three women per company could follow the regiment in campaign). Later it was decided also that only 1/6 of the officers could be married. This right gradually transferred to the Oberste commanders too.

On 1868 the approval for the officers was transferred to the War Ministry, leaving only NCOs and troop under the regiment commander will.

4- the Owner (but one can say the regiment itself) had the right to free his officers and troopers from any bishopric or parish religious duty, holding them only under the regiments-Caplan authority. The reorganization of the military religious branch (1868) abolished this privilege.

5- every member of the regiment gave it the preference in testament's inheritances.

6- in the case of death of one officer without heirs, all the inheritance came to the Owner tax free, apart of the so called Douceur (one horse or 100 Ducats). Abolished in 1769.

7- the Owner had the right to free the leave permissions (freien Beurlaubung) but in many cases this caused a lot of troubles causing its early abolition with the September 1, 1704 Patent.

8- the Owner had the right to impose his personal directives on duties, about service and military exercises. This was suspended on 1737 (March 1) by the Emperor Carl VI with the publication of the common infantry arrangement (Regulament und Ordnung nach welchem Unsere gesamte Infanterie in denen Handgriffen und Kriegsexercitien ....), which came from the 1728 personal arrangement of Fieldmarshal Rogal's regiment.

9- the Owner had the right to establish the uniform of his regiment. This right lasted till 1690 and on 1708 were adopted common uniforms for the army. The Owner actually retained only the privilege to choose the regimental colours (i.e. collars etc.). From 1767 also the colours were chosen by Hofkriegsrat, while the Owner could dress the colours of the musicians. From 1822 they lost also the musicians privilege and the whole uniform became a national matter.

10- the Owner had the right to donate new flags to his subordinate units. These honorary flags, however, had to be left at home.

11- the Owner was the absolute administrator of the regiment. He was helped by the Obristlieutenant and the Obristwachtmeister only the regimental cash management (Cassa). The regimental "properties" of the owner were those stated in the supply-orders sheets (Verpflegs-ordonnanzen). He had a personal supply of 50 man (as mouths to satisfy - Mund) and 12 horse (Pferd) rations per months (the captain, owner of the company, received 15 man and 3 horses portions) in winter (in summer the half). These were retained also if the Owner became the career of General officer. From 1769 all the Owners become generals, also if not in active duty, received yearly an "Inhabers Gage". This ceased in 1798. On 1805 the Owners (as the Oberste commanders and the Staff officers) lost every kind of personal ownership (Staff companies) receiving only the common wages (or Pension) for their rank.

Rittmeister

Cavalry captain (chief of a squadron) since the beginning of the XVII century (note that, till the end of the XVIII century the Dragoons retained the term Hauptmann for theirs squadrons commanders)..

Historically the Rittmeister was the officer charged to give orders (manoeuvres) to a Compagnie zu Pferde (Horse Coy). While his rank was similar to the Hauptmann (captain) the Rittmeister was rather different:

1- the word was an Eastern german word which had to substitute the latin Kapitän (in 1400-1500 the Captains or Condottieri often were not a model of Chivalry); i.e. this Prussian origin is confirmed by the Polish word Rotmisztr. Later the Rittmeister commanded Squadrons as a direct derivation from the Medieval Companies.

2- The Rittmeister was always considered more than a common captain. He had to know horses and had to be expert of Remounts (?) (Remonten), horse sets / saddles and food for horses. For this, the first Rittmeistern were all landowners expert in horse management.

The captain ranks differentiated in three german words (Hauptmann = infantry; Kapitan = Navy; Rittmeister = Chivalry or cavalry).

Rüstmeister
Master of the equipment (Rüstung). See Capitaine d'armes.

Secretär (Regiments-Secretär)
He was mainly employed to manage the regiment's mail traffic, intervened in the records of the regimental order-books and finally was the regiment's historyteller in peace and in war. At the beginning of the XVIII century his jobs were transferred to the Auditore.

Sergeant
The word came from the French term Sergent (it from the Lat. Med. serviens = servant). This term was not popular in the german armies. During the last years of the XVI century (Netherlands war), till the Thirty-years war, every Fähnlein (company) had also 2-3 Sergeanten, in a rank which stood between Feldwebel and Corporal. They were, above all, merely employed as squad commanders (Corporalschaften).

Spielleute
Each Landsknechts companies (Fähnlein) had four (sometimes only two) drummers, called Trommelschläger and after Tambours, plus two pipers (Querpfeifer). They played battle musics near the regimental flags and behind the Fähnrich. A unit formed by one Tambour and one piper was called a play, "Spiel", and the musicians "Spielleute". They also had parliamentary tasks (Parlamentärs-Diensten) when was necessary to directly contact the enemies in the battlefield, expecially the Tambours. Since 1771, in peacetime, they acted also as Lieutenants and Fähnrich orderlies. With the 1806 Regulations the pipers were abolished in the battle formations, remaining only in the regimental bands (Musik-kapellen). As

Mannshaft der Regiments-Musik
they indicated the musicians (and the music apprentices, Musik-Eleven, who could begin the service at the age of 14, but had to enroll only at the age of 17) of the regimental band, instructed by a Kapellmeister or simply by the Regiments-Tambours (from 1896 also Regiments-Hornisten with the Feldwebel rank)

Stabsführer
What made the Profoß in field, made the Stabsführer in camps and barracks. He was appointed to the disciplinary matters. There were one Stabsführer per regimental Staff and one per each Ersatz-bataillone-Cadre (depot or regular recruits training unit later called Kader). The latter was also employed in the depot's administration. In war-time there were eight Stabsführern, one of which had the charge of wagons (baggages) director (Regiments-Wagenmeister), one that of battle Train commander (gefechts-Train), one that of Supply column commander (Proviantcolonne) while the remaining were employed in the escort to the ammunitions' columns and prisoners.

Stellvertreter
Stellvertreter in the literal sense is just a function, a replacement, i.e. a "stellvertretender Regimentskommandeur" would command the regiment whenever the real commander was absent.
In the conscription business, however, if someone was to become a soldier, in some states he was allowed to hire someone else as a replacement: this man would have been a Stellvertreter as well.

Tambour (Regiments-Tambour) (Trommelschläger)
The Charge became official during the Spanish war of Succession, in some regiments. They came from the company Tambours and had to stay in the center of the regiment. The other Tambours were subordinated to him. He had to teach the regimental cadence, the signals for the communications, also with foreign troopers, and the drum management. At camps they provided the drums had to be put in "pyramids" and guarded at the Flag Guard (Fahnenwache). He could

also be sent on parliamentary duties during campaigns. On 1769 this Charge was established in every regimental Staff, with a monthly wage. With the constitution of the Hautboisten bands he acred as the Senior NCO, until he reached the Feldwebel rank (1858). There were also Bataillons-Tambours and Bataillons-Hornisten, who had a rank either of Corporal, either of Gefreyte and who, in peacetime, were in the companies lists.

Unter-Arzt
(see under Ärzte).

Unterlieutenant
Practically a second Lieutenant. On 1701, with the birth of the Grenadiers, these elite troops companies lost the Fähnriche, who became a kind of second lieutenant. It was stated to call the former Lieutenants as Oberlieutenants, while the newbies, the former flagmen, were named Unterlieutenants. See also Lieutenant).

Unteroffiziere für den Sanitäts-Hilfsdienst
Charges assigned only in war-time. These ranks appeared later in the XIX century (1861). They were NCOs commanding the Blessiertenträger Abteilungen (medical stretchbearers sections) and were subordinated to the Regiments-Chefarzt. Every regimental Staff had one Feldwebel and one Corporal per battalion, who acted as medical service NCOs. In wartime the number of the Corporals and that of the Blessiertenträger (three in peace time) doubled. In the Staff there were also eight Bandagenträger (medical orderlies, two per battalion), who carried the sanitary equipments and flanked the "Doctors" in the battlefield.

Vormeister
An artillery Gefreite (see).

Wachtmeister-Lieutenant
The same as Regiments-Adjutant (see Adjutant)

Waffen Offiziere (Regiments – Bataillons -)
The Regiments-Offizier was responsible of the weapons management, organized the participants to the periodic firearms shooting trainings at the army schools and instructed the Bataillonswaffenoffiziere, who were responsible of the control on the hand weapons of the battalion.

Wagenmeister
He had the control on the Train and the baggage of the regiment; he had also to organize the regiment's supply traffic. He was helped by a Fourier, who could eventually subtitute him inr the Charge (Stellvertreter). Otherwise he had a NCO rank and, till 1769, he had to manage the regiment's supply as the official sutler (without being taxed for this job). Since 1722 this Charge was maintained only in war-time when a NCO (generally a Führer) was ordered to handle the Charge, subordinating himself to the Proviant-Offizier. Gradually this system was changed and later a Staff NCO (a Stabsführer) relieved the task as part of the Regiment's Staff and retained the same denomination: Wagenmeister. He controlled the Train columns, the order of the carriages and the personnel (the civil personnel had to dress a mandatory yellow-black arm band).

Werbbezirk Revisor
Later became the Ergänzungs-Bezirks Offizier. Was not part of the regimental Staff. He led the military district office for recruitment.

Zimmermann
A particular kind of Gemeine soldier, free from military basic duties as guards a.s.o., was the Zimmermann (a kind of carpenter) or a soldier expert of manual work and skilled in repairing various things ("Werkzeugen ausgerüstet mann"). This rank was created at the end of the XVII century. Since 1769 till 1807 the Zimmerleute had a rank formerly higher than the Gemeine's one, but had the same pay. There was one of them in each company (two in wartimes). This rank was abolished on 1867 and they were transferred to the Pioneers corps.

Zugsführer
(see Führer)

NOTES

1   Jacob, Nicolas Austrasian, Diete imperiale, ou Ordonnance et resolution de l'Empereur et des estats du S. Empire, Paris 1571, BL 9315aa3, (courtesy of Jeff Lewis, NapSeries).

2   Someone said that the Feldwebel, as the organizer of the coys manoeuvres, in a translate sense, was the "battlefield weaver" (Feld Weber) or the operational arm of the Captain. The modern branch of ranks underlined the administrative skills as a Feld Wiebel. Of course Grimm also has something to say about "weben" (see link below), which could mean "to weave" and also "to move around" (only in the intransitive sense), goes back to an old German verb "weibôn" (= to move around) and is related to Sanskrit "vēpate" (to wabble, to vibrate). But I believe the direct etymology of Weber having developed into the Webel is just a fancy story. First you have got old texts from the 16th century (see the quotes by Grimm) which definitely speak of the Feldweibel (by the way, note the correct spelling), and not a single occurence of a Feldweber, nor of any weaver called Weiber or Weibel. Second, as far as I know as a non-germanist, it is quite unusul in the history of German language that "l" and "r" should be exchanged and a "Weber" becoming a "Webel". Still, also the roots of the Weibel seem to lie in this old German verb "weibôn" and further back in the common indo-european idiom. (courtesy of Oliver Schmidt, NapSeries).

3   (Mark ... I leave to you this translation) ...1808 Fourierschütz Montur: graumelierten kurzen Rock mit schwarzen Kragen, graue Beinkleider, einen runden Hut mit Messingschild auf welchem die Regiments-nummer angebracht war. Die Privatdiener waren wie the gemeiner Fusiliern adjustiert, nur trugen Sie keine Rüstung, nur Tornister und Brodsack und, seit 1810, keinen Schako.

4   In some "ethimos" also from fuorunga, fuarunga (food), vuorunge, where furung = narung, the food-finder. From the ancient hunter slang was who, knowing the places (the guide), brought the hunters scuad directly onto the prey to be killed.

5   Even the State. In 1733 there were five regiment each with five coys payed by Vienna.

6   The word comes from the Lat.Med. *battuere* (to beat), an old word in Latin, but almost certainly borrowed from Gaulish base *bhau-* (to strike) (also in the Welsh *bathu* [beat]; Old.Eng. *beadu* [battle], *beatan* è[to beat], *bytl* [hammer, mallet]). It generated the italian *Battaglia* (with the meaning of company) (also present in the Spanish *Batalla* or *Tercio*) and the 1600 French word *Bataillon*. In the medieval and renaissance armies of the latin countries some companies (*battaglie*) made a Battalion, instead of the regiment. In the german traditional armies the basic units were the Regiment and the Company. The word Battalion appeared later (early 1700), as a normal evolution of the europeans armies.

7   This utter subdivision of an army, since 1637 had the French name of *brigade* (in Italy, *brigata* from It.= *brigata* or harassing troop, quarreling crowd, gang). (Note: many authors in Italy did made a bit of confusion among the Medieval Latin, heir of the Roman language, and the Italian Vulgar, popular, language). The words: *brigare* (to brawl, to fight) and *briga* (strife, quarrel) are all but Latin words. They seems to be instead Italian Vulgar terms with a celtic root. (cf. Gael. *brigh*, Welsh *bri*, word which means power; or the gothic *brikan* - to break and the "*brech, brechen*" of germanic origins). Dante used the word and its verb with the meaning of (generic affair = *briga*) (to do something sometimes in a frenzy and busy way = *brigare*). From these origins came the terms *brigare* for tricky actions and quarrels, *brigante* (brigand) was the hostile litigant. It is difficult to imagine a feudal General officially naming his troops as a brigade (group of brigands). It is rather strange an utter splitting of the divisions could be named with a not Latin (the language of nobles and clergymen) word. Discussion's open. At least, utter sources put the Brigadier's birthday in 1678, hence after the birth of the French brigade (1637).

Brigade, moreover, was a French term. Its meaning was that of a group of armed men who went into the battle with the *brigandine* (*une espece d'armure de fer dont les brigans estoient armez, faite à lames estroites, qui consent aux courbeures et plieures du corps de l'homme qui en est armé*), a sort of armor made of thin horizontal bands, which allowed the soldiers movement, being not rigid because of its joints. The Roman armor called *Lorica laminata*. Here a enlighting text. All began when the City of Paris sent its troops onto the war: "*La ville de Paris offrit pour la ville et vicomté 600. glaives et 400. archers, et mille Brigands, et pource que ces gens de pied allans et venans à la guerre, pilloient le peuple, on a prins ce mot pour un larron de campagne, un voleur de pays, qui exerce le brigandage és chemins et voyes publiques*». The brigands, so, were originally irregular soldiers armed with every kind of rural weapon meeting together in momentary bands (brigades), who mantained themselves by pillages, robberies and crimes. These last particular behaviour granted the modern meaning of brigands. It is possible, hence, that a group of soldiers, larger than a regiment, momentary organized, provisional, not trained to act together, could be named as Brigade.

8   French *pionnier*, from Old French *peonier*, foot soldier, and from Med. Lat. *Pes-Pedis* (foot), roots *pedō, pedōn-* one who has broad feet, from Late Lat. *pedonarius* (marching area), *pedestris* (afeet). Translate meaning into "people who march afeet, poors, not riders" (Span. *peon*), with the extension to indicate the workers who preceded the cavalrymen in order to execute works on the battlefield (or more properly who worked to raise the wooden installations in the Tournament's places. For someone the word could originate from the Old. Fre. *Pic(onnier)* (Sp. *piconeiro*, It. *Picconiere*), stones breakers, workers with the pick, who made roads (Med. Ned.*pike- pikke*).

Bildliche Darstellung

DER

K. K. Oesterreichischen

ARMEE.

Lithographirt und zu haben bey Jos. Trentsensky in Wien.

THE
COLOUR
PLATES

FROM THE WORK OF JOSEPH TRENTSENSKY

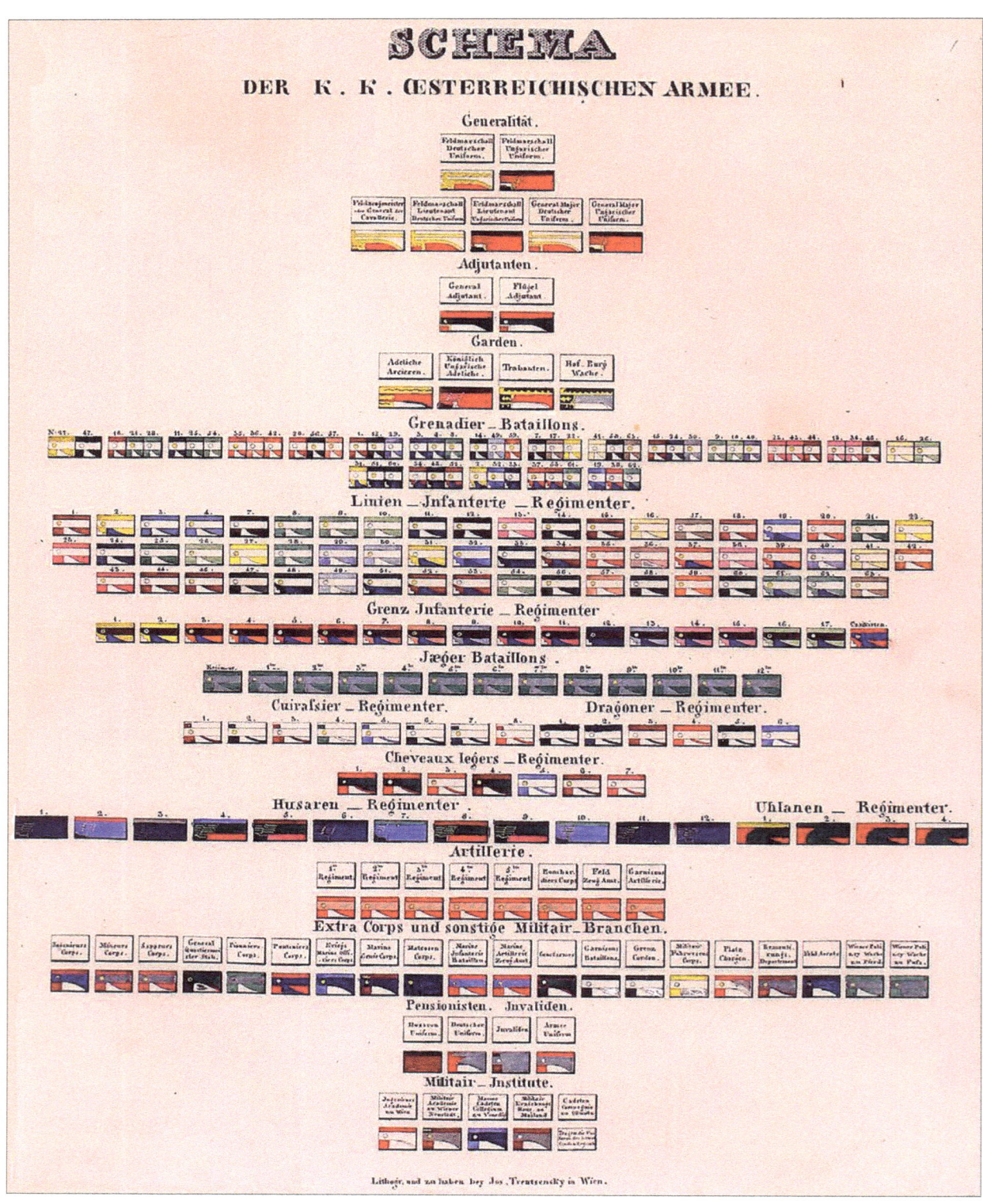

▲ Schema of color uniform for the Austrian imperial & royal army

K.K. Oesterreichischer General der Cavalerie und General Adjutant

Austrian Cavalry General and general Adjutant

K. K. Oesterreichischer General Major.

Austrian Superior General

K. K. Ungarischer General Major.

Lithog. und zu haben bey Jos. Trentsensky in Wien.

Hungarian Superior General

Jk. Ik. Adelige erste Arcieren-Leibgarde.

First Archer of Guard du corps

Königl: ungar: adelige Leibgarde.

Lithogr. und zu haben bey Jos. Trentsensky in Wien.

Hungarian Officer of Guard du corps

Royal trabants of Guard du corps

K.K. Oesterreichische Hofburgwache.

Austrian Hofburg palace Guard

Austrian Grenadiers

K. K. Ungarische Grenadiere.

Lith. und zu haben bey Jos. Trentsensky in Wien.

Hungarian Grenadiers

K: K: Oesterreichische Linien Infanterie.

Lithogr. und zu haben bey Jos Trentsensky in Wien

Austrian line infantry

K. K. Ungarische Linien Infanterie.

Hungarian line infantry

41

K. K. Österreichische Gränz Infanterie.

Lithogr. und zu haben bey Jos. Trentsensky in Wien

Austrian Grenzer infantry

K. K. Österreichische Jäger

Lithogr. und zu haben bey Jos. Trentsensky in Wien.

Austrian jager

43

K. K. Oesterreichische Landwehr.

Lithogr. und zu haben bey Jos. Trentsensky in Wien.

Austrian Landwehr

44

Jr. K. Oesterreichischer Cuirassier Officier.

Lithogr. und zu haben bey Jos. Trentsensky zu Wien.

Austrian Cuirassier Officer

45

K. K. Oesterreichischer Cuirassier.

Lythogr. und zu haben bey Jos. Trentsensky in Wien.

Austrian Superior General

K. K. Oesterreichischer Dragoner Officier.

Lithogr. und zu haben bey Jos. Trentsensky in Wien.

Austrian Dragoon Officer

Kₖ. K. Oesterreichischer Gemeiner Dragoner.

Austrian Dragoon

K. K. Oesterreichischer Chevauxlegers Officier.

Lithogr. und zu haben bey Jos. Trentsensky in Wien.

Austrian Chevauleger Officer

N: 53. Oesterreichischer Chevaux-Legers.

Leipzig, und zu haben bey den Terwesalk Wien

Austrian Chevaulegers

K.K. Österreichischer Husaren Officier.

Lythogr. und zu haben bei Jos. Trentsensky in Wien.

Austrian Hussar Officer

Austrian Hussar

K.K. Oesterreichischer Uhlanen Officier.

Lithog. und zu haben bey Jos. Trentsensky in Wien.

Austrian Hulan Officer

K. K. Oesterreichischer Gemeiner Uhlane.

Lythogr. und zu haben bey Jos.Trentsensky in Wien.

Austrian Hulan Lancer

K.K. Oesterreichische Artillerie.

Austrian Artillery

55

K.K. Oesterreichischer Ingenieur Officier
und Cadet der Ingenieur Accademie in Wien.

Lithog. u. zu haben bey Jos. Trentsensky in Wien

Austrian Engineer Officer and cadet

K. K. Oesterreichische Mineurs.

Austrian Miners

K.K. Österreichische Sapeurs.

Austrian Sapper and Officer

58

K. K. Generalquartiermeisterstab.

Lithogr. und zu haben bey Jos. Trentsensky in Wien.

Austrian General of major Staff

K. K. Oesterreichische Pionniers.

Lithogr. und zu haben bey Jos. Trentsensky in Wien.

Austrian Pioneer and Officer

K.K. Oesterreichische Pontoniers

Lithographirt und zu haben bey Jos. Trentsensky in Wien

Austrian Pontoneers

K. K. Oesterreichischer Marine Genie Corps Officier und Cadet.

Lithogr. und zu haben bey Jos. Trentsensky in Wien.

Austrian Navy Engineer Officer and cadet

Ih. K. Oesterreichisches Matrosen Corps.

Austrian navy sailor and officer

K. K. Oesterreichische Marine Infanterie.

Lithogr. und zu haben bey Jos. Trentsensky in Wien.

Austrian Navy Infantry

K. K. Oesterreichisches Marine Artillerie Corps.

Lithogr. und zu haben bey Jos. Trentsensky in Wien.

Austrian Marine Artillery Corp

K.K. Oesterreichische Czaihisten.

Austrian Czaipristen

K. K. Oesterreichischer Stabs Dragoner Officier

Lithogr. und im Lehen-Verlag der Trentensky in Wien.

Austrian Staff Dragoon Officer

K: K: Oesterreichischer Gemeiner Stabs Dragoner.

Lithogr. und zu haben bey Jos. Trentsensky in Wien.

Austrian Private Staff Dragoon

K.K. Gemeiner der italiænischen Gensdærmerie zu Pferd.

Lithogr. und zu haben bey Jos. Trentsensky in Wien.

Private of Italian gendarme at horse

K.K. Italianische Gensdarmerie

Lithogr. und zu haben bey Jos. Trentsensky in Wien.

K.K. Italian gendarmes

K.K. Oesterreichische Garnisons-Bataillon u. Grenz Cordons Gemeine

Austrian Garrison battalion and Private Grenzer

K: K: Oesterreichisches Militair Fuhrwesen Corps.

Lithogr. und zu haben bey Jos Trentsensky in Wien

Austrian Military Furnish Corp

K.K. Oesterreichisches Beschäl und Remontirungs Departement

Lythogr. und zu haben bey Jos. Trentsensky in Wien

Austrian Bescahl Departzment

K. K. Oesterreichischer Platz Officier und Stabs-Feld Arzt.

Austrian garrison Officers

K. K. Oesterreichischer Regiments Caplan und Feld-Kriegs-Comissair

Austrian Chaplain and Field War Commissar

Wiener Gendarme at horse

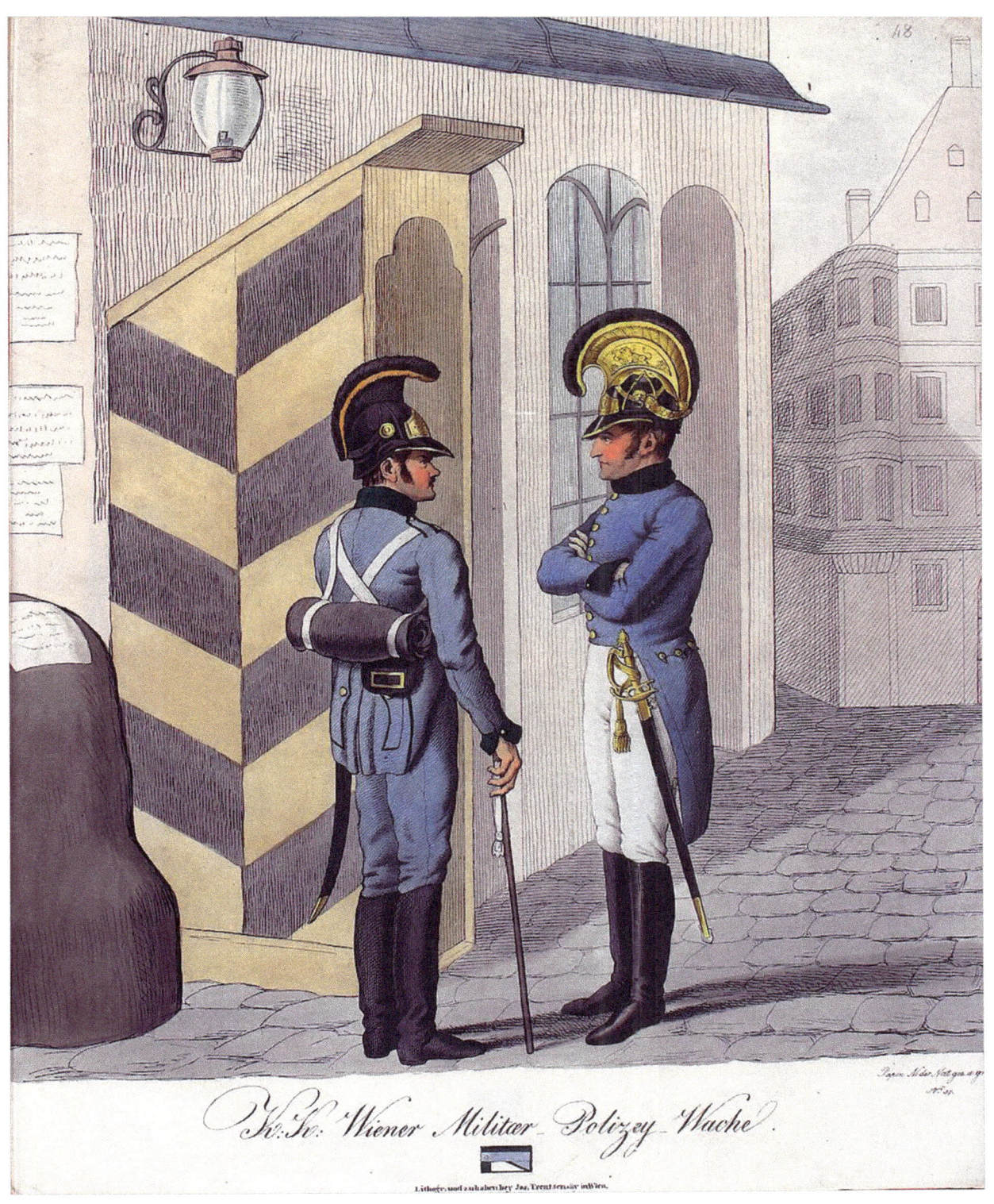

K. K. Wiener Militær-Polizey-Wache.

Wiener Gendarme at foot

K. K. Oesterreichischer Invalide, und

Regiments Erziehungs Knaben.

Lythogr. und zu haben bey den Trentsensky in Wien.

Austrian Invalid and young Cadets

K. K. Oesterreichische Pensions Officiere

Lithogr. und zu haben bey den Trentensky in Wien.

Austrian Invalids

Officier und Zögling der k.k. Oesterreichischen Militair Academie zu Wiener-Neustadt.

Lithogr. und zu haben bey Jos. Trentsensky in Wien.

Military Accademia of Wiener-Neustadt

APPENDIX
COLOUR
PLATES

FROM THE WORK OF RICHARD KNOTEL

AND OTHERS 1797-1815

Corps der Akademie der bildenden Künste.   Aufgebot der Vorstädte.

Corps des Handlungsstandes.   Universitäts-Corps.

Wiener Freiwillige.
1797.

Austrian Wiener Volunteer Infantry 1797

Landständisches Corps. Im Hintergrunde Landsturm. Berittenes Corps.

Volksaufgebot in Nieder-Oesterreich.
1797.

Austrian Reserve Land troops 1797

Ungarischer Grenadier.   Deutsche Grenadiere.

1799.

Austrian and Hungarian infantry 1799

Offizier
vom Bat. Nr. 11.

Soldat
vom Bat. Nr. 9.

Leichte Infanterie.
1798—1801.

Austrian Light Infantry 1798-1801

Jäger-Regiment zu Pferde Graf Bussy.
1798—1801.

Jaeger at horse Regiment Graf Bussy 1801

Leichtes Dragoner-Regiment Levenehr Nr. 14.

Slavonisch-Kroatisches Grenz-Husaren-Regiment (Nr. 12).

1798—1801.

Dragoon of 14th reg and Grenzer Hussar 1798-1801

K. K. Infanterie-Regiment Hoch- und Deutschmeister.
1805.

Infantry Regiment Hoch and Deutschmesiter 1805

Deutscher Grenadier.   Deutscher Infanterist.   Ungarischer Grenadier.

1813.

Austrian and Hungarian Infantry 1813

Kürassier-Regt. 1. Kaiser Franz.

1813.

1st regiment of Cuirassier Kaiser Franz 1813

Huszaren
vom Huszaren-Regiment Fürst Liechtenstein.
1813.

Private of Hussare reg. First Liechtenstein 1813

Infanterie der Deutschen Legion.

1813—14.

German Legion Infantry 1914

Austrian Infantry 1805 (by Gerash)

Austrian Dragoon 1805 (from Viskuezzen collection)

Austrian Jaeger at horse 1805 (from Viskuezzen collection)

Austrian Hussar 1805 (from Viskuezzen collection)

Austrian Hussar 1805 (from Viskuezzen collection)

Austrian Hussar 1805 (from Viskuezzen collection)

Austrian Hussar 1805 (from Viskuezzen collection)

SOLDIERS, WEAPONS & UNIFORMS ALREADY PUBLISHED
(SELECTION TITLES)

UNIFORMS OF RUSSIAN ARMY IN THE ERA OF ANCIENT TZAR
FROM THE REIGN OF VASILI IV TO MICHAEL I, ALEXIS, FEODOR III DURING THE XVII th CENTURY
A.V.VISKOVATOV   LUCA STEFANO CRISTINI
SWU-600-004

UNIFORMS OF RUSSIAN ARMY OF PETER I THE GREAT
FROM THE REIGN OF PETER I TO CATHERINE I, PEER II, ANNA AND IVAN VI. 1682-1741
A.V.VISKOVATOV   LUCA STEFANO CRISTINI
SWU-700-006

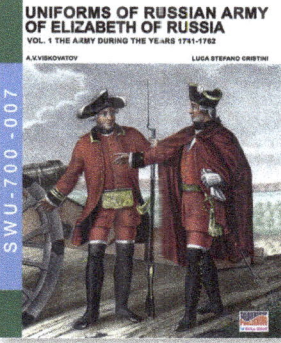

UNIFORMS OF RUSSIAN ARMY OF ELIZABETH OF RUSSIA
VOL. 1 THE ARMY DURING THE YEARS 1741-1762
A.V.VISKOVATOV   LUCA STEFANO CRISTINI
SWU-700-007

UNIFORMS OF RUSSIAN ARMY OF ELIZABETH OF RUSSIA
VOL. 2 THE ARMY DURING THE YEARS 1741-1762
A.V.VISKOVATOV   LUCA STEFANO CRISTINI
SWU-700-008

UNIFORMS OF RUSSIAN ARMY IN THE XVIII CENTURY VOL. 1
UNDER THE REIGN OF CATHERINE II EMPRESS OF RUSSIA BETWEEN 1762 AND 1796
A.V.VISKOVATOV – LUCA STEFANO CRISTINI
SWU-700-005

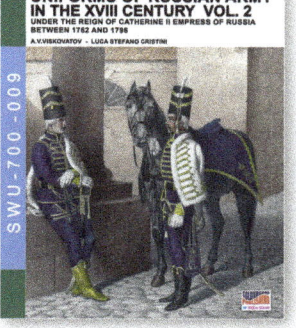

UNIFORMS OF RUSSIAN ARMY IN THE XVIII CENTURY VOL. 2
UNDER THE REIGN OF CATHERINE II EMPRESS OF RUSSIA BETWEEN 1762 AND 1796
A.V.VISKOVATOV – LUCA STEFANO CRISTINI
SWU-700-009

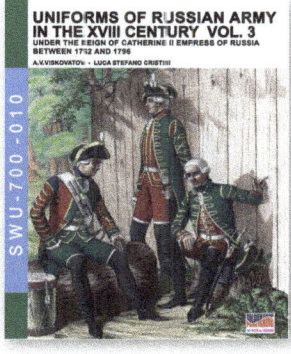

UNIFORMS OF RUSSIAN ARMY IN THE XVIII CENTURY VOL. 3
UNDER THE REIGN OF CATHERINE II EMPRESS OF RUSSIA BETWEEN 1762 AND 1796
A.V.VISKOVATOV – LUCA STEFANO CRISTINI
SWU-700-010

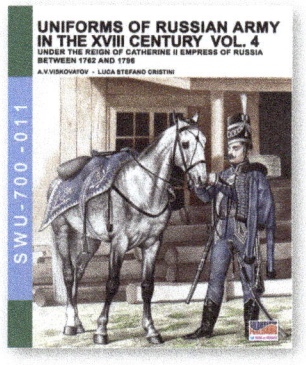

UNIFORMS OF RUSSIAN ARMY IN THE XVIII CENTURY VOL. 4
UNDER THE REIGN OF CATHERINE II EMPRESS OF RUSSIA BETWEEN 1762 AND 1796
A.V.VISKOVATOV – LUCA STEFANO CRISTINI
SWU-700-011

BRITISH ARMY UNIFORMS IN 1742
IN THE ART OF JOHN PINE
SWU-700-001

UNIFORMS OF RUSSIAN ARMY OF ELIZABETH OF RUSSIA
VOL. 2 THE ARMY DURING THE YEARS 1741-1762
A.V.VISKOVATOV   LUCA STEFANO CRISTINI
SWU-700-008

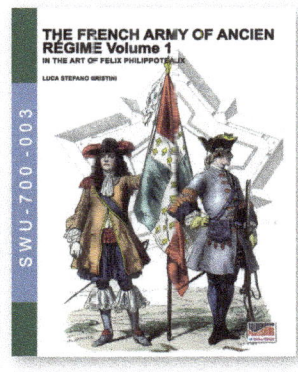

THE FRENCH ARMY OF ANCIEN RÉGIME Volume 1
IN THE ART OF FELIX PHILIPPOTEAUX
LUCA STEFANO CRISTINI
SWU-700-003

THE FRENCH ARMY OF ANCIEN RÉGIME Volume 2
IN THE ART OF FELIX PHILIPPOTEAUX
LUCA STEFANO CRISTINI
SWU-700-004

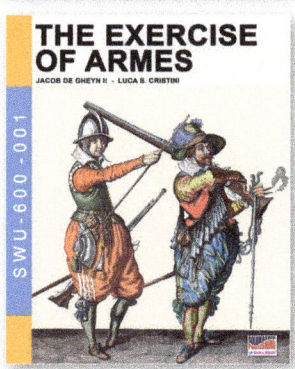

THE EXERCISE OF ARMES
JACOB DE GHEYN II. - LUCA S. CRISTINI
SWU-600-001

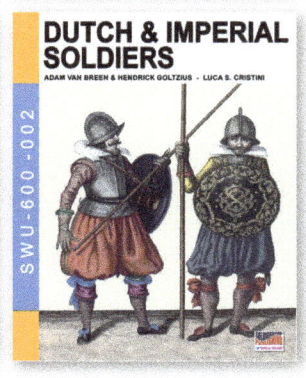

DUTCH & IMPERIAL SOLDIERS
ADAM VAN BREEN & HENDRICK GOLTZIUS - LUCA S. CRISTINI
SWU-600-002

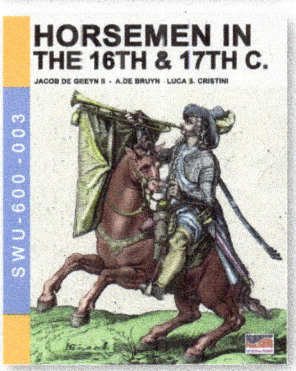

HORSEMEN IN THE 16TH & 17TH C.
JACOB DE GHEYN II - A.DE BRUYN - LUCA S. CRISTINI
SWU-600-003

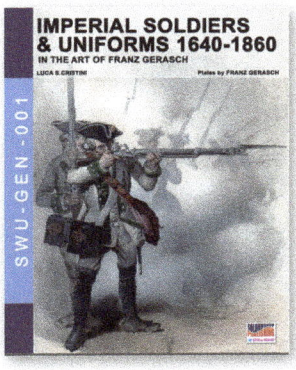

IMPERIAL SOLDIERS & UNIFORMS 1640-1860
IN THE ART OF FRANZ GERASCH
LUCA S CRISTINI   Plates by FRANZ GERASCH
SWU-GEN-001

www.ingramcontent.com/pod-product-compliance
Lightning Source LLC
Chambersburg PA
CBHW041146120626
46547CB00020B/3129